DIARY

OF A

MINECRAFT

ZOMBIE

Book 3

Zack Zombie

Sunday

ow!

I can't believe it.

Mom and Dad just told me that they're taking us to the Jungle Biome for Spring break!

The Jungle Biome is like the coolest biome ever.

Best of all, it's got the best Amusement Park in the entire Overworld.

It's called "Creepy World," and it's awesome.

They've got the best minecart rides.

They've got the Wicked Twister and the Head Ripper.

And, they have the scariest ride ever known to zombie-kind called The Zombie Thrasher.

Man, it's going to be the best Spring break ever.

The only thing I have to worry about is that my little brother is coming too.

I was trying to tell my Mom and Dad that little brothers aren't allowed in Creepy World, because it may give them permanent brain damage.

But I think it backfired, because they got really excited after I said that.

Then I tried telling them that they didn't have rides for little kids. It was all for 7 year old kids and above.

But they started talking about the "Zombie Minion Madness Ride" and the "It's A Small Zombie World" ride.

They even said that there's an entire section of Creepy World for kids called "Zombie Kiddieland."

I was out of ideas, so I guess the little wart is coming to Spring break scarecation with us after all.

But, I don't care because it's going to be the best Spring break ever!

Monday

All the kids at school were talking about where they were going for Spring break.

As soon as I told them I was going to the Jungle Biome, their eye sockets got real big and their jaws dropped. Some of them even started drooling.

I finally started to get some respect in the classroom.

That was until Big Mouth Jeff opened his mouth and told everybody he was going to the Ocean Biome.

He said that his family was going to spend a week at the Ocean Monument Hotel and Amusement Park.

All the kids forgot about me and started gawking and drooling at Jeff.

Something tells me that Jeff is making it up, though.

I mean, Zombies aren't supposed to be able to breathe underwater.

But who knows. He probably has an uncle that invented some kind of underwater Zombie suit that helps zombies breathe underwater. And I bet that Jeff has like three of them.

Some Zombies get all the breaks.

I asked Skelee, Slimey, and Creepy where they were going for Spring break.

"I don't know yet," Skelee said.

"Me, either," Slimey said.

"I'm going to find out this week," Creepy said. "But I just hope it's not the Jungle Biome. The way you talk about it, it sounds really scary."

"It sure would be cool if we could all go to the same place for Spring break," I said. "Then we can have all kinds of fun together."

"You should tell your Mom and Dad to call our parents. That way we can all go to the Jungle Biome with you," Skelee said.

"That sounds awesome!" Slimey said.

But Creepy didn't like that idea.

We finally got him to come by promising him that we wouldn't let him get on any scary rides.

But somehow we convinced him to go to the Haunted House.

Go figure...

Man, this Spring break scarecation is turning out to be the best scarecation ever!

Tuesday

I walked my ghoulfriend Sally to school today.

I asked her if she wanted to come to the Jungle Biome with me and the guys for Spring break.

But she said she had to go with her Mom and Dad to their house in the Snow Biome.

"Wow, your parents have a house in the Snow Biome?"

"Yeah, we have a house in just about every Biome," Sally said.

"Wow, your parents must be rich," I said.

"Yeah, my Dad made a lot of money during the last Zombie Apocalypse," she said. "His company supplies armor for the Zombie Army."

"Whoa, that's cool."

"Yeah, it pays the bills," she said.

"But aren't you afraid of Snow Golems?" I asked her. "The kids at school say that they're worse than Iron Golems."

I told her how one time, a kid at school had an uncle that got caught by some Snow Golems. They used his head and his limbs to play a game of snow baseball. If an ice cream truck hadn't come by, he would've never escaped.

"Oh silly, those are only stories," she said. "Snow Golems only bother us if we go next to the human village. Our house is way on the other side of the mountain."

"Oh, OK," I said.

I told her about my plans, and about Creepy World, and about the Zombie Thrasher, and about my little brother, and the guys coming to Jungle World with me, and about my mom taking me to get new clothes, and…

Man, I thought Sally was the one that talked a lot.

Wednesday

Today our Scare Class took a trip to go see some cave bats.

I think cave bats are dumb.

All they do is fly around and make noise.

But they don't do anything cool, like Killer Rabbits, or Ghasts and stuff.

But anyway, we went through some caves to find the bats, but we didn't find any.

So me and the guys decided to do some cave exploring.

Ms. Bones let us go exploring as long as we followed her one rule, "Don't bother the cave spiders. You know how upset they can get."

Me, Skelee, Slimey, and Creepy went into this really dark cave.

"HISSSSSS." I could already hear Creepy getting nervous.

But we saw a light up ahead, which calmed him down.

The light led us to an abandoned mineshaft. It actually looked like somebody was recently working there.

"Hey, this reminds of a movie I saw last night," Skelee said. "It was called Indiana Bones and the Temple of Doom."

"It was really cool. The best part was when Indiana Bones jumped into a minecart and rode really fast like a rollercoaster," Skelee said.

"Hey, there's a minecart," I said. "Why don't we jump in?"

All of us jumped into the minecart and pretended we were on a giant rollercoaster.

"Man, this is what it's going to be like at Creepy World. It's going to be so awesome," Slimey said.

"Guys, I don't feel so good…" Creepy said.

"Aw, just sit in the back of the cart if you feel queasy," we told him.

"Oh, OK."

Creepy went to sit down, but as soon as did, his foot kicked the brake lever.

"Hey, we're moving!"

All of a sudden the minecart went up through a few caves until we reached the top of the mountain, then "Whhhooooosssshhhhh!!!!"

"AAAAAHHHH!!!!" we all screamed.

The minecart was going about a hundred miles an hour down the mountain and through the caves and all around the abandoned mineshaft.

"AAAAAAHHHHH!!!!" we kept screaming.

"Hey, where's Creepy?" Slimey asked.

We looked at the back of the minecart, and Creepy was gone!

All of a sudden we heard a loud, "BOOOOOMMM!" from where we came from.

"Oh, No…You don't think?" Skelee said to me with a worried look on his face.

I just looked at him scared.

Then all of a sudden we slowed down as we came to the end of the mineshaft.

"Oh, Man. What are we going to tell Creepy's parents?" Skelee said.

"I don't know," I said.

We all walked back to Ms. Bones' class, with our heads hanging low.

When we got to Ms. Bones' class, she scolded us for taking so long.

"Ms. Bones. We have to tell you something... It's about Creepy..." I said.

All of a sudden Creepy came out of nowhere and said, "Hey guys, how was the minecart ride?"

Me, Skelee, and Slimey just stood there with our mouths open.

"What's the matter?" Creepy asked.

"We thought you blew up! What happened to you?"

"Well, as soon as the minecart started moving, I fell out. Actually, I got lost. I accidentally ran into a cave full of TNT. Then I… Uh… accidentally activated one. If it wasn't for the cave spiders I would've been blown up for sure," Creepy said.

"How did you escape?"

"Well, the cave spiders covered me in spider webs. It stopped the blast from hurting me. Then I rode the cave spiders all the way back here," he said.

"Well, I'm just glad you're OK," I said.

Skelee sighed and said, "Man, I wish I could ride a cave spider."

Thursday

Today Mom took me to get some new school clothes and some clothes for our trip to the Jungle Biome.

I was really excited.

I wanted to get some of the coolest clothes that the kids at school were wearing.

Well, everything was going great until I found out that Mom decided to take us to Creep Mart to get my new clothes.

I was hoping she was going to take me to "Scarget," or "Old Scary Navy." Even "Rabies R Us" would've been better than Creep Mart.

Then when we got there, Mom went ahead and picked out all of my clothes and made me try them on.

16

"Mom, I look like a dork!" I said, after looking at myself in the mirror.

"But I thought that's what all the kids at school are wearing nowadays?" she said.

Man, Moms don't know anything about picking out cool clothes.

Slimey's Mom bought him some new school clothes this year, and on the first day of school, all of the mob kids laughed at him.

I laughed too. I couldn't help it.

Slimey really tried to rock those parachute pants, but it just didn't work.

Another time, Skelee's Mom made him wear jeans with stripes on them. All the kids said they made him look really skinny.

Well, I'm not going to let that happen to me. No way!

"Mom, I'm twelve years old. I'm old enough to pick out my own clothes," I said.

"You're right, honey," she said. "Oh, my little Zombie is growing up so fast." Smmmaaccckkk! She kissed me in front of all the people at the store.

So embarrassing…

Then I picked out some clothes that I thought would really make me look cool.

"Yeah, just right," I said as I looked in the mirror.

My Mom kinda looked at me funny, but she didn't say anything because she knows I'm a big Zombie now.

And afterward we went to get cookies and ice cream.

Friday

Man, it was awful.

As soon as I got to school, everybody was staring at my new clothes.

Nobody was saying anything, so I thought, they must love my new "duds."

Then one kid started laughing, and soon everyone else started laughing too.

My worse daymare came true.

Worst of all, I had to walk around school all day with these clothes on.

At lunch, Slimey and Skelee came by to see me, and they gave me a nod like they could understand what I was going through.

"Man, I don't get it," I said. "I was sure these were the clothes that all the cool kids at school are wearing."

"Naw, those are the clothes that the cool kids at school are wearing." Skelee pointed at Big Mouth Jeff as he walked into the lunchroom.

I was so confused. Everything I thought about the universe came crashing down at that moment.

When I looked at Big Mouth Jeff, he was wearing the same outfit my Mom had picked out for me.

Life is so unfair.

Saturday

Today, I was going to ask Mom to take me back to the store, so I could exchange my clothes.

But I felt like if I did that, then she would use it as an excuse to pick out my clothes till I was thirty.

So I didn't say anything.

I just had to get rid of these clothes before Mom made me wear them again.

So I had an idea.

I went to visit Mutant at his house, but when I got there, he wasn't home.

But I didn't go to find Mutant anyway.

As soon as I got there, I took out my new clothes and put them in a bucket. Then I poured out the largest bottle of carrot juice I could find all over them.

Then I stuck some twigs in them so that they looked like me.

I started making noise like I was walking around, when all of a sudden, Fluffy the Killer Rabbit came out.

I wasn't sure if Fluffy would take the bait, so I started saying mean things like Mutant's older brother: "Why are you playing with those rabbits, you dumb Ogre? Urrghh, Urrghh, Urrghh!"

All of a sudden, Fluffy's eyes grew bright red and he tore my little stick zombie statue apart.

Man, I've got to remember never to make Fluffy mad at me.

When Fluffy was finished with the clothes they looked like spaghetti.

I quickly put them on, because I was going to go home and tell Mom I got attacked by a Killer Rabbit.

But then, Fluffy came out again…

Oh, Man, I thought. I think he wasn't finished yet…

His beady little eyes glowed red, and I was sure I was dead.

Then all of a sudden, Fluffy jumped on my head and rubs his face next to mine.

Whew! That was a close one.

Well, I guess when my Mom smells me now, she'll really think I got attacked by a Killer Rabbit.

When I got home, I told my Mom and Dad that the Killer Rabbit attacked me again.

It worked like a charm. I even got Mushroom milk and cookies for all my troubles.

My Mom took me to the store to get more new clothes.

"You know, Mom," I said. "I don't show you enough appreciation. I think I'm going to follow your advice on what clothes I should wear."

My Mom was so happy that she bought me an extra shirt.

Man, it's good to have a Killer Rabbit around when you need one.

Sunday

I went to go see Steve today to tell him about my plans for Spring break.

I found him in some caves playing with some TNT.

"BOOOOOOMMM!!!"

I went in to check on him, but all I found were his tools floating around the cave.

Next thing I know, Steve comes into the cave.

"How did you?... But you were?... Never mind," I said.

I was so excited to tell Steve about my plans I didn't have time to ask him how he did that disappearing trick.

"Hey, guess what?" I said. "I'm going on scarecation with my parents to the coolest biome ever!"

"What's a scarecation?" Steve asked.

"A scarecation is when you skip school to go someplace fun with your family… You know, scarecation," I said.

"Ohhhhh. We have those too. We call them vacations," Steve said.

Vacations? Why would anyone go somewhere to vaca? I thought.

"Anyway, me and my family are going to the Jungle Biome for Spring break. Isn't that awesome?" I said.

"That's really awesome," he said. "And guess what?"

"What?" I said.

"I'm going to the Jungle Biome too!" Steve said. "I was planning on exploring the Jungle Temple about the same time you're going."

"Wow, that's great! I'm trying to get Skelee, Slimey, and Creepy's parents to go too. Man, we're all going to be there together."

"Do you guys want to go exploring in the Jungle Temple with me?" Steve asked. "It's supposed to be the resting place of the Wishing Emerald."

"What's that?"

"Well, the Wishing Emerald is supposed to make anything you wish for come true. I'm not sure it's real, but I want to go explore the Jungle Temple to see if I can find it," Steve said.

"Count me in," I said. "That sounds awesome."

So I walked away thinking about how our Spring break is going to be ten times better, now that Steve's coming.

Also, the Jungle Temple sounded tight.

Man, this is going to be the most amazing Spring break ever...

Monday

I saw all the guys at school today, and they told me they were all coming to the Jungle Biome!

"Thanks for having your Mom and Dad call our parents," Skelee said.

"Guess what?" I said. "Steve is coming to the Jungle Biome with us, too."

"Whoa, that's awesome! But what are your parents going to say?" Slimey said.

"Oh, actually he's just coming to explore the Jungle Temple, and he asked us to come too."

"Man, that sounds tight! I heard the Jungle Temple is like the scariest place in the Jungle Biome," Skelee said.

"I hope it's not too scary," Creepy said.

"Steve said he's looking for the Wishing Emerald that makes your wishes come true," I said.

"Whoa…" everybody said.

"Slimey, you can wish for a new pair of parachute pants," Skelee said.

We all burst out laughing.

"I'm going to wish that I wasn't so scared all the time," Creepy said.

"I'm going to wish that I can breathe under water. I always wanted to visit the Ocean Biome," Slimey said.

"I'm going to wish for an enchanted bow and arrow," Skelee said. "What are you going to wish for, Zombie?"

"I don't know yet. But I'm going to make it big."

"Coooool," all the guys said.

Tuesday

I saw Mutant at school today.

He was busy rebuilding the gym because he accidentally destroyed it after our last Dodge Ball game.

"Hey, Mutant!" I said.

"Uuurrrrggghhh!"

"It's good to see you too," I said.

"Hey, I wanted to see if you wanted to come with us to the Jungle Biome for Spring break. All the guys are coming, and I wanted you to come too."

"Uuurrrrggghhh!"

"Really? You can't come?"

"Uuurrrrggghhh!"

"You have to spend Spring break rebuilding the gym?"

"Uuurrrrggghhh!"

"And you don't have any clothes to wear, anyway?"

"Man, that's a bummer," I said. "It would've been really great if you could come. I wanted to introduce you to my human friend, Steve. He's real cool. I think you would like him."

"Uuurrrrggghhh!"

"How does he taste?!!"

"Uuurrrrggghhh!"

"Oh, what is his grade?"

"I think he's in middle school like us, but for humans."

"Uuurrrrggghhh!"

"Yeah, I think he's cool too," I said.

RRRIINNNGGGG!

"Oh, there's the bell. I've got to get to my class. I'll see you later, Mutant."

"Uuurrrrggghhh!"

Mutant gave me his finger to give him a high five, but this time he gave me a high five.

I had to pick my arm off the floor and run to class so I wouldn't be late!

Wednesday

Today at school, we had a special guest speaker.

He came to speak to us about Mob safety.

I guess they must've heard about our minecart ride from our last field trip.

I think the guy must've been from the Zombie Police because he was really stiff.

His name was Officer Ricky D. Bones.

He talked about how we need to stop doing all the usual stuff...

You know, no going out during the daytime, no playing with torches, no tipping over spiders, no bothering silverfish, NO RIDING MINECARTS, no getting close to Golems...

You know, all the fun stuff us mob kids really like to do.

He especially said that we should stay away from humans, because they can be real dangerous. He even said that humans have medicine that can cure all the cool diseases that we have. So we should stay away from them.

The last thing he said was, "I would hate any one of you to become human."

Wow, I didn't know humans can turn Zombies into humans… That's insane.

I need to ask Steve about that one.

Come to think of it, I wonder if Zombies can turn humans into Zombies?

Whoa! I wonder who would know that?

I thought I could ask Mom and Dad, but I changed my mind because they might think I want to be human like Steve.

I decided to ask the witch that lives in our neighborhood.

I know she's retired now, but I'm sure in her younger days she used to turn humans into Zombies, or frogs or something.

So after school, I went to the witch's house.

"What do you want?" she said when she opened the door.

She answered the door with that mean look on her face.

I tried to answer, but I just couldn't stop looking at her big nose with a mole on it.

"Uh… Ms. Witch…Um, I had a question for you," I said. "Today at school I learned that humans can turn Zombies into humans. I was wondering… Can Zombies turn humans into Zombies?"

"They sure can… All it takes is one bite from a Zombie to turn a human into a Zombie," she said.

All of a sudden she started to cackle, "AHAHAHAHAHAHAHAHA!"

I also think I heard some lightning and thunder in the background, and even the lights flickered a little bit.

"Can they ever turn back?" I asked her.

"Yes, but only with the most powerful magic," she said. "The only witch I know who has that kind of magic lives in the middle of the Swamp Biome, and she can only be found during a full moon."

"Really?"

"Yes, and you would never want to go visit her, because she has a particular taste for rotten flesh. AHAHAHAHAHAHA!"

Again with the cackling. Sheesh.

"Why are you asking, anyway?" she asked me as she gave me her evil eye.

"Just curious," I said. Then I said good bye and walked away.

"Goodbye. AHAHAHAHAHAHA!!!"

Wow. No wonder she doesn't have any friends.

Thursday

Me and the guys decided to go to the Zombie Cafe next to our school for lunch today.

They sell all kinds of food there.

Some of the kids at school say that the place is really clean, which kinda made me a little nervous.

41

But, they also said that the place is full of rats and bugs, which made me feel better.

The real reason I go there is because they have my favorite food in the whole world... Cake!

I got a big, giant cake and I was going to eat the whole thing.

But I could see that Skelee didn't bring any money with him, plus he was looking really skinny lately.

"Want some cake?" I asked Skelee.

"Naw, thanks," he said. "Cake usually goes right through me."

"I could use some Mooshroom Milk though. My Mom says it's full of Calcium."

I gave Skelee a few bucks and he got himself a carton of Mooshroom Milk.

As he drank it, I was a bit confused about how he gets the Calcium part.

Creepy got himself some Pop Rocks.

Kinda made us all nervous every time he ate some.

Slimey got a mucus shake.

It was green, because I think it was Mint flavored.

"I really like coming to the Zombie Cafe," I said. "They have the best food."

"Yeah, me too," Skelee said. "It sure beats the Chinese restaurant next door, The Woking Dead."

"My favorite restaurant is Drool and Gruel," Slimey said.

"I like Bombastic Pizza," Creepy said. "Me and my family always go there."

I didn't know how I felt about that...

Friday

I'm so excited about Spring break!

One more week and we're going to be knees deep into the Jungle Biome.

I just got a Zmail from the guys telling me about all of the stuff they're going to bring.

Skelee is bringing his Indiana Bones hat.

Slimey is bringing his parachute pants. "At least this way they don't have to go to waste," he said.

Creepy was bringing his new Liquid Nitrogen Inhaler. He said it was the latest thing for keeping Creepers calm in scary situations. His Mom got it for him from the Bomb Supply store.

45

"It even works if a Creeper gets struck by lightning," he said.

Whoa.

I sent a Zmail back telling the guys that I was bringing my climbing shoes for the Jungle Temple.

Zombies are normally good climbers. They can climb ladders and even vines.

But I lost a few toes this week, and Mom said we were fresh out of toes from our body parts stash in the basement. So she had to put ears on my feet until we could order some more body parts.

So my climbing skills are not so good right now.

I have to figure out what to do about my pet squid while I'm gone, though.

I could give him to the witch down the street, but I'm afraid when I get back my pet squid will grow a big nose and start walking and talking.

Whoooooohhhh. That's just creepy thinking about it.

I know what I'll do. I'll just set him free in the lake next to the village.

47

I'll tell Mom and Dad it escaped.

Maybe this way I can get a cooler pet...like a Killer Rabbit.

Saturday

Today, Mom had the brilliant idea that before I can go on Spring break, I had to do something about my dirty room.

I usually don't do anything about my room for eleven months out of the year, so in the Springtime my Mom gets on my case about it.

"You need to do something about this room, young man. Or you can forget about Spring break," My Mom said.

But I like the way my room looks.

I mean, I know that I have dirty clothes lying around all over the place...

And I know there's moldy food under my bed that attracts bugs...

And I know I have plenty of my dirty underwear and smelly gym socks hanging on all of the furniture...

But Mom says that it's not good enough. She thinks I can do better.

She told me to get some of last week's left over garbage, and dump it in my closet.

She even told me to sprinkle more maggots in my drawers.

Urrrrgghhh! Taking care of my room is such a pain!

After my room, Dad wanted me help him with the garage too.

It's not even a garage anymore.

My Dad turned it into his own Zombie Cave.

Which makes me wonder why I have to help him with it.

I guess he thinks I want to inherit it when he's gone.

But I think it's kinda lame.

Right now my Dad has his hobby Abandoned Mineshaft and Minecart Rail set in there.

He also has a Zombie Apocalypse set with Zombie and Human action figures, which I kinda like... But he won't let me play with it, so it's lame.

Now, if he were to put in a 70 inch TV with a video game chair that comes with vibrating seats, then I would gladly help him with it.

But he wants my help adding more cobwebs, dust, and dirt to his Zombie Cave. He even wants me to help him add cow poo compost bedding for the floor.

Uuuurrrgghh! I hate Spring chores.

Sunday

I went to go visit Steve today.

I wanted to ask him what humans do for Spring break.

I found him punching trees again today.

I still don't know how he does that without losing any fingers.

"Wassup, Steve!"

I guess this time he saw me coming, because he wasn't surprised.

"Wassup, Zombie!" Steve said.

"Hey, did you hear me coming or something?"

"Naw, I actually smelled you before you got here," he said. "You're kind of extra ripe today. Cough, cough…"

"Thanks, Man, I've been working on that. But anyway, I had a question for you about humans."

"Hit me," he said.

So I smacked him on the back of the head.

"What'd you do that for?!!"

"You told me to hit you, didn't you?" I said.

"Forget about it. What's your question?"

"Hey, what do humans do for Spring break?" I asked.

"Oh, Man. We do really cool stuff for Spring break, but the best place to go for Spring break is Disneyland," Steve said.

"Disneyland? What's that?" I asked.

"Disneyland is a magical place, where kids of all ages can go on exciting rides, spend time with life-sized characters like Mickey Mouse, Donald Duck, and Goofy; eat corn dogs on a stick, and spend time with hundreds of other people, along with their family and friends."

"Whoa, that sounds really scary. Giant Mice, giant ducks, giant dogs. Eating dogs that are stuck on a stick. And all of those humans in one place… Dude, you're freaking me out!" I said.

"There's a ride I think you would really like, though. It's called The Haunted Mansion. It has Zombies and Ghost attacking humans and everything," he said.

"Oh. I guess humans aren't so bad," I said. "If I ever visit you again, let's go there."

"Sure, man." Then Steve went back to punching his tree.

I wanted to ask Steve if it was true that humans can use medicine to turn a Zombie human. But I didn't want him to think I wanted to become human or something, so I didn't ask.

I did walk away thinking that maybe humans aren't as bad as Officer Bones said they were.

With places like the Haunted Mansion around, how bad can they be?

Monday

I looked in the mirror this morning and I noticed that something was growing on my chest.

It looked fuzzy with a green and blue color to it.

"Dad, Dad! Come in here!" I yelled.

"What is it, son?"

"Dad, what's this green stuff growing on my chest?!!"

"Congratulations, son, you're growing mold on your chest," he said. "That means you are going through puberty."

"Poo—ber—tee? What's that? Does that have something to do with poo?!!"

"No, son. Puberty is when a young Zombie starts to become a big Zombie."

"Soon you'll have mold growing on your chest, back, under your arms, and your face. I even have it growing out of my ears," Dad said.

"I'm going to have it growing out of my ears? Eeeeeww, gross!"

"Don't worry son, you'll get used to it," Dad said. "Though it does get a little itchy when the bugs lay their eggs in it."

"Also, son, you're going to see other changes as you go through puberty."

"Like what?" I asked.

"Well, your feet are going to get bigger, so you may feel a little clumsy at times," he said. "And one foot usually grows bigger than the other."

"Whoa."

"Also, son, your voice is going to start to get deeper," he said. "Then you'll be able to say UUUUURRRRGGGHHH! Just like your Dad."

"Let me try… Uuuurrgghhsqueeeekkk!"

"Yep, you're definitely going through puberty," Dad said.

"Here, son, you're going to need this." Dad handed me a small bottle.

"Pro-odor-ant ." I tried to read it. "What is it, Dad?"

"Well, son, sometimes puberty can make things happen that you don't want. Like you're going to start to smell different," he said.

"What!"

"Yeah. You're going to lose some of that nice, pungent, rotten flesh smell," he said. "So you may have to use some Pro-odorant so that it isn't noticeable."

"Man... Puberty is hard."

"Don't worry. You'll get used to it," he said. "It happens to all of us."

Man, I bet this stuff doesn't happen to Skelee, or Slimey.

And what about Creepy? How is he going to grow mold when he doesn't even have arms?

I bet Steve doesn't have to go through this either.

Wow... It really stinks to be a Zombie.

Hey, maybe I won't need the Pro-odorant after all...

Tuesday

Kids in middle school really like to swear a lot.

They come up with some of the weirdest swear words I've ever heard.

Today, one kid called another Zombie a really bad swear word, and it almost started a fight.

Now, I don't normally use swear words. But I keep a list so if I ever have to, I'll be ready.

Also, I thought I would preserve a historical record of the common expletives of adolescent Zombies for the benefit of future generations.

Naw, just kidding. I really like to collect them because I think they sound so funny.

So far I've heard Zombies called:

Dead Head
Meat Bag
Slack Jaw
Gutter
Shuffler
Brainless
Moanie
Screecher
Biter
Chiller
Thriller
Meat Puppet
Rotter
Floater

And the worst of all the worst swear names I have ever heard someone call a Zombie…

"Brain Muncher!"

Yuck! That's like the worst thing you could ever call someone.

Even thinking about it gives me the creeps.

I just have to make sure my Mom never gets a hold of my journal…

Wednesday

Today I had my Zombie Karate class test.

It was real intense.

The Zensei told us that we were going to be judged on form, power and technique.

I was really nervous, but I knew I could do it.

I started my technique and it was awesome.

I could tell I lost a few points for form. It was probably because of my clumsy feet.

Then I had to be tested for power.

I had to break three wooden slabs with my feet, and then break three wooden slabs with my hand.

I psyched myself up real good, and then I went for it.

Hyaaaaahhhhh!

Crack!

My foot went flying halfway across the room.

It ended up hitting Creepy on the head really hard.

All the kids ran for cover, and some kids even dived out the window.

But Creepy used his Liquid Nitrogen Inhaler today, so it wasn't a big deal.

Well, that didn't go too well. But I was determined to ace my hand board break.

I hobbled over to the wooden slabs that were on top of the cobblestone blocks.

I pulled my arm back and I gave it all I've got.

64

Hyaaaaaahhhhh!

Pop, pop, pop, pop, pop!

All my fingers broke off and flew in different directions.

I think one hit a classmate in the eye socket, because it went in his direction, but then it disappeared as soon as it hit his face.

Man, I thought, I'm going to fail my karate test.

"Not today!" I said to myself. So I went for it again.

Blam!

I broke the boards so hard they shattered to pieces.

I even had a piece stuck to my forehead.

"Congratulations. You passed your test," Zensei said. "Good job using your head."

I was so happy I passed my test.

But boy, my head really hurts.

Thursday

Today Dad was telling me how much he wants us to spend some quality time camping together when we go to the Jungle Biome.

He said that getting back to nature would be great for us.

Also, he said it would help me get an appreciation for the outdoors, the way our ancestors used to live.

"Dad, I thought our ancestors lived in caves?" I asked.

"Yes, son. But they went out every night to enjoy the night air. And that's what we're going to do," Dad said.

Hey, I like camping as much as the next Zombie, but I was really looking forward to

67

hanging out with my friends during our Spring break adventure in the Jungle Biome.

But, I guess I can do it for one day.

"OK Dad, I'll go camping with you for ONLY ONE DAY of our scarecation," I said.

"Great, I'll start packing our gear. This is going to be the best family scarecation ever!" he said.

Well, it was going to be...

Before bed, Mom asked me to read a bed-time story to my brother.

She was busy getting ready for a presentation for work or something.

So I chose the scariest book I could find.

I thought, maybe I could scare my little brother and he'll be so traumatized, Mom will

68

have to leave him with Grandma for Spring break.

So I grabbed the most diabolical book ever created called, "There's a Kid Under My Bed."

I remember when Mom read this book to me when I was a kid. I had daymares for weeks. I even stopped wetting the bed for a whole month.

I thought, this should really scare the "bejeezus" out of my little brother.

Half way through reading the book, my little brother fell asleep.

He wasn't scared at all.

Man, when I was a kid, this book terrified me. Why didn't he get scared?

It must be something they put in the water or something, I thought.

Later, in the middle of the day, I heard the loudest scream I had ever heard.

When I woke up, I went to my little brother's room and he was rolled up in a ball at the corner of his bed.

Mom and Dad rushed in the room and held my little brother to calm him down.

"Mamma, Dadda... Dares a liddle kid hiding unda my bet!!!!"

Mom looked at me with that piercing look that told me I was in real trouble.

Man, I was sure it would work...

Friday

Today was our last day before Spring break.

Everybody at school was so excited to finally get a break from school.

I went around saying goodbye to everybody.

Sally had left a day early, so I said goodbye to her yesterday.

I was just really happy that my best friends were coming with me to the Jungle Biome.

Me, Skelee, and Slimey all jumped on Mutant, because we all wanted to say goodbye to him at the same time.

Creepy didn't. I think Creepy is still scared of Mutant.

Mutant smiled and gave us all a big hug.

Later, Creepy called our parents to come pick us up.

Took them a while to find all of our body parts and stuff...

When I got home, I put myself back together and finished packing for my trip.

I was so excited!

I made sure I packed all of the essentials:

Comic books—Check.

Snot and boogers for snacks—Check.

Dirty underwear—Check.

Stinky feet spray—Check.

Zombie Diary (I mean Journal)—Check.

I also brought some climbing gear so I can go explore the Jungle temple with Steve.

Man… This is going to be the best scarecation ever!

Saturday

By the time we arrived at the Jungle Biome, it was almost daytime.

We went straight to the hotel to get some sleep and get ready for the next day.

We're staying at the Bat Cave Hotel.

It's dark, dingy, and dirty—It's awesome!

Tomorrow we're going to Creepy World. I'm going to meet all of the guys there.

Right now I'm so excited I can't even sleep.

Tomorrow, I'm going to ride the Wicked Twister, the Head Ripper, and I'm going to be the first in line for the Zombie Thrasher.

I also can't wait to go to the Haunted House!

They say they have real humans there.

Can't wait!

Sunday

Man, today was the worst day ever!

I can't believe it, but my Mom and Dad made me go to "Zombie Kiddieland," to spend time with my brother.

"But Mom!" I said. "All of the guys are going to the amusement park to ride The Head Ripper and Zombie Thrasher! I'm going to miss it all."

"Well, if they're your real friends, they'll wait till tomorrow to go with you," she said. "Today we're going to spend time together, and bond as a Zombie family should."

How could this happen?

Everything was so perfect. Now my entire scarecation is ruined because my Mom and Dad want to "bond" as a family.

This stinks.

But, I guess it wasn't all bad.

Creepy's family was in Zombie Kiddieland too.

He doesn't have a little brother. He's just too scared of the big Zombie minecart rides.

We did have fun riding on some of the kiddie rides.

It kind of reminded me of when I was a kid and I used to go to the amusement park with Mom and Dad.

Plus, it was kind of nice "bonding" with my Mom, Dad, and little brother.

It was lame…but nice.

I guess I can wait one more day to spend time with all the guys.

And I know my friends; they wouldn't go without me.

I asked my mom to borrow her cellphone so I could call the guys to see what they were up to.

"Don't use it too long," Mom said. "My Redstone battery is running out."

"Hello?" I said.

All I could hear on the other end was, "WHOOOAAYYEEEAAAHHHH!!!!"

"Skelee? Slimey? Where are you guys?" I said.

"WHOOOAAYYEEEAAAHHHH!!!!" They said. "DUDE, THIS IS AWESOME! THE ZOMBIE THRASHER IS THE BEST MINECART RIDE EVER!!!!! WE'LL CALL YOU BACK LATERWWHHHOOOAAAAAHHH!!!

So much for loyalty.

Monday

The guys told me that since they went on the minecart rides like five or six times yesterday, they wanted to do something different today.

I was bummed.

But I felt better when the guys decided to go to the Haunted House.

At least this way we can all go, even Creepy.

I was a little worried for Creepy (and mostly for us). But Creepy said he brought his Liquid Nitrogen Inhaler in case he got nervous.

The Haunted House didn't look that creepy on the outside, but as soon as you walked inside, it was the scariest thing you ever saw.

They were playing a scary movie called "Harry Potter" and it was the most terrifying thing I had ever seen.

We walked into another room, and then a giant plant came out of the ground to chomp on Zombies as they walked through the room!

It was the Zombie eating plant from that terrible video game Steve lent me.

All of the guys and me were screaming like little girl Zombies.

The only one who was surprisingly not affected was Creepy.

I thought, man, that Inhaler must be working!

We walked into another room and there was a little Zombie girl sitting in the middle of the room playing with her dolls. Then when we got up close to her, she jumped at us.

And she had a human face!!!!!!

We were so scared we almost crushed each other as we tried to escape.

The next room looked like an Insane Asylum, except there was blood everywhere and hooks hanging all over the place.

Everything looked normal until…

Two people came in. One looked like a Zombie doctor and the other a patient. The patient sat down in a chair, and then the doctor took out a drill…and…and…

The doctor started fixing the patient's teeth!

Scariest thing ever!

The doctor started laughing, and when he took off his face mask, and he had a human face too!

By this time I hurled all the cake I had eaten for lunch.

Slimey broke into his medium Slimey bits after the first room, and now he was down to his miniature Slimey bits… I'm not sure if he'll be able to put himself back together after this one.

The thing that sent Skelee over the edge was when he saw them putting skin back on one of the Skeletons.

I've never seen Skelee that scared. I think that was his worst daymare come true.

But Creepy... He just kept smiling and walking along. I could not understand what was up with him.

The last room is going to haunt me for weeks...

It was a mineshaft full of Zombies, Skeletons, and Creepers, just minding their own business and having some fun.

All of a sudden, a bunch of diamond Miners with pickaxes and swords started attacking all of the mobs!

Creepers were blowing up all over the place!

Skeletons were getting cut down to pieces and dropping bones everywhere.

The Skeletons were so freaked out they were accidentally shooting Creepers and blowing them up.

There was rotten flesh, bones, music discs, and giant craters all over the place.

By this time, we almost lost it.

We ran out of there as fast as we could.

I think I dropped some body parts behind because I felt lighter.

I must've not been the only one, because outside of the Haunted house they had a Lost and Found for dropped items.

There were Zombie body parts, bones, Slime bits, even music discs in there.

And as we left the Haunted House, they played the theme from "Harry Potter."

I think that song is going to haunt me for weeks…

Tuesday

Today we went to the Jungle Gym part of the Jungle Biome.

They had zip-lining, vine swinging, and climbing.

Zip-lining is when you hold on to a pulley that rides a rope between trees.

It was my favorite of all the Jungle Jim rides.

But, boy, when Dad said puberty made you clumsy, he wasn't kidding.

I felt like I was all thumbs.

Even the kid that really had all thumbs did better than me.

Skelee was a natural at it.

Slimey couldn't get the hang of it. I still can't understand why.

But Creepy surprised us all. He was climbing and swinging, and riding the zip-line like he grew up here.

Which was really weird since he didn't have any arms.

Man, that Liquid Nitrogen Inhaler of his must really be working.

Maybe I should borrow it sometime.

The guys got bored of the Jungle Jim, so they decided they wanted to climb the side of a mountain.

I think they didn't see the sign with the Zombie falling off the mountain...

Now, climbing up mountains is a lot harder than it looks.

There aren't any ropes in case you fall, so it was real scary.

Skelee got up the mountain in no time flat.

Creepy got up the mountain real quick too.

But even with my climbing shoes, I felt so clumsy up there.

Uuuurrrrgghhh! I just couldn't get the hang of it.

Then I looked to the side of me and I saw Slimey, paralyzed with fear, stuck on a ledge.

"I want to go home," Slimey said crying.

I felt really bad for him, especially if he fell and broke into Slimey bits. I don't think he would survive a fall from that height.

"I'm coming over there, buddy," I said.

I climbed over to where Slimey was and got a hold of him.

But then I realized that I wouldn't be much help with my terrible climbing skills. And Slimey being paralyzed with fear didn't help either.

All of a sudden, a bat came out of one of the holes in the mountain and it really scared Slimey.

He jumped off the ledge...taking me with him!

"AAAAHHHHH!!!!" We yelled.

I knew I was a goner. My whole 12 year old life flashed before my eyes.

Then, out of nowhere…

Boing………. Boing……. Boing…… Boing, Boing, Boing!

When we stopped bouncing, I was still trying to make sense of what just happened.

"Hey, wait a minute… I thought Slimes take serious fall damage?" I said.

"Well, my Mom made me stuff Slime blocks in my parachute pants," he said. "She was afraid I would fall off a mountain or something."

We looked at each other for a minute and burst out laughing.

Next thing, I see Skelee jump off the top of the mountain.

He landed right on Slimey's parachute pants.

Boing.........................Boing..............
Boing.......Boing....Boing, Boing, Boing!

"Man, this is fun!" Skelee said.

Then I saw Creepy getting ready to jump off too.

"Hey, get up quick, before Creepy jumps off!" I said.

Inhaler or no inhaler, that was an experiment that I didn't want to try...

Wednesday

Today my Dad planned for us to go on a Jungle Biome tour.

I really wanted to go with my friends, but I promised my Dad.

It was supposed to be a night trip into the Jungle Biome, real Dad and son bonding type stuff.

It sounded pretty lame, but it actually turned out to be pretty cool.

Our first stop was to see the giant jungle trees. These things were huge.

They had vines on them, so for part of the tour we were able to climb them.

I climbed all the way to the top of one and the view was epic!

My Dad almost made it to the top but Mom called because my little brother got lost.

Dad spent the entire time on the phone trying to calm her down.

They finally found my little brother playing with the life-sized Elder Guardian character at the Zombie Kiddieland park.

I could see the whole jungle from where I was.

I could even see the Jungle Temple!

That was good because I could give Steve directions when he got here.

After we climbed down, the tour was over. So we got some Cocoa Pods to take home as souvenirs, and we left.

We bumped into an Ocelot, and I wanted to take him home. But Dad reminded me that Creepy was allergic to them, so I didn't.

Overall, it was really fun.

I got some time to bond with my Dad, even though he was on the phone the whole time.

Plus, I found the Jungle Temple, which is great because when Steve gets here, I'll be ready.

I can't wait!

Thursday

Today I finally got a chance to go on the minecart rides at Creepy World.

First ride I tried was the Head Ripper.

It was so intense, a few Zombies got their heads ripped right off.

It was awesome.

One Zombie put his head on backward, and rode the Head Ripper again.

Took his head clean off again, but backward.

Man, I love minecart rides!

Usually the heads just roll down a dumpster and mobs pick them up at the lost and found.

But, one Zombie decided he would ride the Head Ripper standing on his head.

Took his legs right off.

I think he still can't find them.

I guess his legs didn't fit in the dumpster.

But the ride I was really looking forward to was the Zombie Thrasher.

They say that the G-forces on the Zombie Thrasher are so strong that if you're not strapped in, it can rip your rotten flesh right off.

One Zombie rode it, and he didn't strap in because his friend dared him not to, so he came out looking like a Skeleton.

They gave him a toy bow and arrow to keep him quiet.

But I made sure I was strapped in.

Hey, I like living on the edge… But I like my entrails more, thank you.

But riding the Zombie thrasher was awesome!

I even got a free toy bow and arrow too.

I had Skelee pretend like he was me coming out of the ride, and it worked like a charm.

Man, this is the best scarecation ever.

Friday

Tomorrow I'm going to meet Steve to go explore the Jungle Temple.

Man, I'm really excited!

I wonder if there'll be booby traps, and treasure and stuff.

Steve said that he was going to look for the Wishing Emerald, and that it's supposed to give you anything that you wish for.

I wonder what I'm going to wish for...

Maybe I can wish to be taller, like Mutant. Then the kids will really give me some respect.

Or, I can wish to have six arms and legs like a spider. Then I can get all my chores done really fast.

I wonder what would happen if I wished for Creepy to get arms?

Naaa, he probably wouldn't know what to do with them.

Oh Man! I could wish for my little brother to turn into a pet pig, or a pet rabbit, or something!

Naw… Then Mom would be sad and be crying all the time and stuff.

Hey, maybe I could wish to be human. That way I won't have to deal with all the stuff that Zombies go through.

I mean, Steve doesn't look like he has any problems.

Man, that would be the life. All I have to do is punch trees all day, collect rocks, plant vegetables, and mine for diamonds.

You know, I don't know why a Zombie's life is full of so much drama.

But, on second thought, if I was human I would probably miss all of my friends, Mutant, and I would definitely miss Sally.

And I know it sounds lame, but I would probably miss my Mom and Dad too.

Naw. Being human would probably not be fun at all.

I think I'm just going to wish for eyeballs.

Saturday

Today I told my Mom and Dad that me and the guys were going on a full day Jungle Biome Tour.

They wanted to spend time with the other parents so they let us all go.

Me and the guys met up, and we took the tour to the Jungle Biome like before.

I remembered where the Jungle Temple was, so we headed in that direction.

I wasn't sure if I should tell Creepy that there were Ocelots in the Jungle. So I checked to see if he had his Liquid Nitrogen Inhaler with him.

Creepy said he had it, but he said it was almost empty. I decided to keep the Ocelot information to myself.

As soon as we got to the Jungle Temple, Steve was waiting there for us.

"What's happening, fellas?" Steve said.

All the guys gave Steve a high five. Except for Creepy, because he doesn't have arms.

As we were going into the Jungle Temple, there were all these signs around the entrance.

One sign had a skull and crossbones on it.

Skelee thought it was a sign for the bathroom.

"Hey Steve, what does the sign with the skull and crossbones mean?" Slimey asked.

"That means that it's dangerous for humans," Steve said.

"I thought it was a sign for the bathroom," Skelee said. "Man, I really had to go, too."

Steve was still walking in, even though the sign said it was dangerous. Wow, Steve is just one tough dude, I thought.

"Is it dangerous for us?" Creepy asked.

"I don't know, I guess if it was then there would be a few mob signs too," Steve said.

"Makes sense," we all said.

As soon as we walked in, an arrow flew by our heads and hit Steve in the shoulder.

"I think that's why there was a sign outside," Slimey said.

"Hey, Steve, you look just like when we played cowboys and Indians," Skelee said.

"Yeah," said Steve.

As we were walking around we found a big area with walls with lots of vines on it.

Then we walked downstairs into another room, and there were three levers on the wall.

"What are those for?" I asked Steve.

"Those are for finding the secret rooms," Steve said.

"Secret rooms? Whoa!"

"Now, let's see if I know the right order for these," Steve said, as he looked in his little journal.

"You have a diary too? So do I." And I showed Steve my cool Diary/Journal combo.

Steve smiled and pulled a lever.

All of a sudden the ground started shaking and we heard a loud rumbling noise.

He pulled another lever and the same thing happened again.

"OK. This should be the last one," Steve said.

Then we heard another rumbling sound.

"That should do it," Steve said.

We ran upstairs and suddenly there was a secret room open.

"Hey, what are these strange Skeleton markings on the wall?" Slimey asked.

"I can read those! My uncle taught me ancient Skeleton when I was little," Skelee said.

As Skelee was translating the signs, the rest of us went inside and found a chest.

Steve opened the chest, and in it, there was the fattest emerald we had ever seen.

Steve lifted the emerald and he said, "We found it! This is the Wishing Emerald. You can wish for whatever you want and it'll come true."

"Whhooooaaa!" we said.

"What are you going to wish for, Steve?" I asked.

"I'm going to wish for what I've always wanted," Steve said… "I wish I was a Zombie!"

All of a sudden, Steve started shaking and glowing...

And then I started shaking and glowing…

Then just like that, Steve turned into a Zombie that looked just like me!

It was amazing.

But then the guys were all looking at me funny.

"Uh, you should probably look in a mirror," Slimey said.

I pulled out my pocket mirror that I use to keep my hair looking cool. And when I looked in it, I couldn't believe my eyes…

I looked like Steve!

Just then, Skelee ran into the room and said, "I think I know what the symbols mean. It's a warning that whoever uses the emerald to wish for something, that they should be very careful what they wish for."

"Put that thing back, Steve!" I said.

Steve threw it back in the chest, and we ran downstairs, and moved the levers to close it up again. Then we got out of there really fast.

"Oh, Man! What are we going to do?" I said. "I can't go home looking like this! My parents won't let me in the house!"

"You don't look so bad, you know," Steve said. "Uuuurrrgghh!"

"Whatever we do, we can't tell my Mom and Dad," I said. "Steve, that means that you need to go back with my parents. I need to trust you guys to help Steve act like me, so my parents won't notice the difference."

"How are you guys going to turn yourselves back?" Skelee asked.

"Well, I heard about a witch that lives in the Swamp Biome that can turn Zombies back into humans... And I think she can turn humans into Zombies too. But I don't think she comes back till the next full moon, which is a few weeks from now," I said.

"Wow, we get to stay like this for a few weeks? This is going to be fun!" Steve said.

"Let's head back. Remember Steve, you've got to be me for the next few weeks," I said.

"No problem," Steve said with a grin. "I got this."

That night we headed back. Steve went back to the hotel where my parents were. And he gave me a map to show me how to get back to his village.

Oh, Man. I wonder what life is going to be like living with humans for a few weeks.

Well, I guess I'm going to find out…

Find out What
Happens Next in...

Diary of a Minecraft Zombie Book 4
"Zombie Swap"

Get Your Copy and Join Zombie on
More Exciting Adventures!

If you really liked this book, please tell a friend. I'm sure they will be happy you told them about it.

Leave Us a Review Too

Please support us by leaving a review. The more reviews we get the more books we will write!

Check Out All of Our Books in the Diary of a Minecraft Zombie Series

The Diary of a Minecraft Zombie Book 1
"A Scare of a Dare"

In the first book of this hilarious Minecraft adventure series, take a peek in the diary of an actual 12 year old Minecraft Zombie and all the trouble he gets into in middle school.

Get Your Copy Today!

The Diary of a Minecraft Zombie Book 2
"Bullies and Buddies"

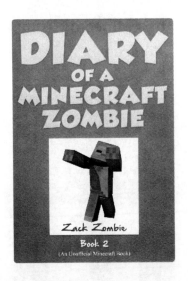

This time Zombie is up against some of the meanest and scariest mob bullies at school. Will he be able to stop the mob bullies from terrorizing him and his friends, and make it back in one piece?

Jump into the Adventure and Find Out!

The Diary of a Minecraft Zombie Book 3
"When Nature Calls"

What does a Zombie do for Spring break?
Find out in this next installment of the exciting
and hilarious adventures of a 12 year old
Minecraft Zombie!

Get Your Copy Today!

115

The Diary of a Minecraft Zombie Book 4
"Zombie Swap"

12 Year Old Zombie and Steve
have Switched Bodies!
Find out what happens as 12 year old
Zombie has to pretend to be human and
Steve pretends to be a zombie.

Jump into this Zany
Adventure Today!

The Diary of a Minecraft Zombie Book 5
"School Daze"

Summer Vacation is Almost Here and
12 Year Old Zombie Just Can't Wait!
Join Zombie on a Hilarious Adventure as
he tries to make it through the last few
weeks before Summer Break.

Jump into the Adventure Today!

The Diary of a Minecraft Zombie Book 6
"Zombie Goes To Camp"

Join 12 year old Zombie, as he faces his
biggest fears, and tries to survive the next
3 weeks at Creepaway Camp.
Will he make it back in one piece?

Jump into His Crazy Summer Adventure and Find Out!

The Diary of a Minecraft Zombie Book 7
"Zombie Family Reunion"

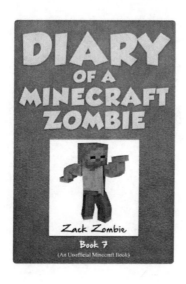

Join Zombie and his family on their crazy
adventure as they face multiple challenges
trying to get to their 100th Year
Zombie Family Reunion.
Will Zombie even make it?

Get Your Copy Today
and Find Out!

The Diary of a Minecraft Zombie Book 8
"Back to Scare School"

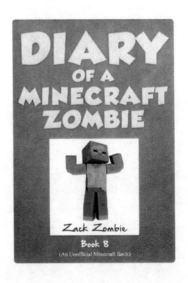

Zombie finally made it through 7th grade...
And he even made it through one really crazy
summer! But will Zombie be able to survive
through the first weeks of being an 8th grader
in Mob Scare School?

Find Out in His Latest Adventure Today!

The Diary of a Minecraft Zombie Book 9
"Zombie's Birthday Apocalypse"

It's Halloween and it's Zombie's Birthday!
But there's a Zombie Apocalypse happening that
may totally ruin his Birthday party. Will Zombie
and his friends be able to stop the Zombie
Apocalypse so that they can finally enjoy some
cake and cookies at Zombie's Birthday Bash?

Jump into the Adventure
and Find Out!

121

The Diary of a Minecraft Zombie Book 10
"One Bad Apple"

There's a new kid at Zombie's middle
school and everyone thinks he is so cool.
But the more Zombie hangs out with him, the
more trouble he gets into. Is this new Mob kid
as cool as everyone thinks he is, or is he really a
Minecraft Wolf in Sheep's clothing?

Jump Into this Zany Minecraft Adventure and Find Out!

058296931

CPSIA information can be obtained
at www.ICGtesting.com
Printed in the USA
LVOW08s2005070517

533643LV00010B/34/P